Dear Parent:

Congratulations! Your child is taking the first steps on an exciting journey. The destination? Independent reading!

STEP INTO READING® will help your child get there. The program offers five steps to reading success. Each step includes fun stories and colorful art. There are also Step into Reading Sticker Books, Step into Reading Math Readers, Step into Reading Write-In Readers, Step into Reading Phonics Readers, and Step into Reading Phonics First Steps! Boxed Sets—a complete literacy program with something for every child.

Learning to Read, Step by Step!

Ready to Read   Preschool–Kindergarten
• big type and easy words • rhyme and rhythm • picture clues
For children who know the alphabet and are eager to begin reading.

Reading with Help   Preschool–Grade 1
• basic vocabulary • short sentences • simple stories
For children who recognize familiar words and sound out new words with help.

Reading on Your Own   Grades 1–3
• engaging characters • easy-to-follow plots • popular topics
For children who are ready to read on their own.

Reading Paragraphs   Grades 2–3
• challenging vocabulary • short paragraphs • exciting stories
For newly independent readers who read simple sentences with confidence.

Ready for Chapters   Grades 2–4
• chapters • longer paragraphs • full-color art
For children who want to take the plunge into chapter books but still like colorful pictures.

STEP INTO READING® is designed to give every child a successful reading experience. The grade levels are only guides. Children can progress through the steps at their own speed, developing confidence in their reading, no matter what their grade.

Remember, a lifetime love of reading starts with a single step!

*To Zach, who renews his
motorcycle license year after year*
—S.E.G.

*To Wyatt, Jay, and Lilliana,
the next generation of West Cornwall babies*
—M.J.D.

Acknowledgments: Our thanks to Emilio Scotto of Around the World Enterprises, Perry Michael of Perry Michael Designs, Sam Wheeler, DaimlerChrysler AG, Tim Jordan, Ducati Motors, and Riders for Health for providing pictures. And thanks to Knievel Custom Cycles for letting us use the dramatic picture of Robbie Knievel jumping the Grand Canyon.

Cyndi Cohen helped organize our amazing ride through Gettysburg with her friend Jen Le Van, owner of Battlefield Harley-Davidson, and Jen let us photograph her motorcycle-loving dog. Bob Paolella, Sr., of Brothers' Harley-Davidson in Branford, Connecticut, not only provided the Dyna Wide Glide 2006 but also modeled a helmet.

Finally, special thanks to Heidi Kilgras and Christy Webster, whose patience and enthusiasm are extraordinary.

Photo credits: cover: © Royalty-Free/CORBIS; pp. 3, 11, 21: © Ducati Motors; pp. 4, 6: courtesy of Robbie Knievel; p. 5: © Bettmann/CORBIS; p. 12: © Stu Forster/Allsport; p. 13: courtesy of Emilio Scotto; p. 16: © Mercedes-Benz Classic; p. 17: © Markus Cuff/CORBIS; p. 25: © Riders for Health; p. 26: © Peter Blakely/CORBIS SABA; p. 29: © George Grantham Bain Collection; p. 30: © US Department of Defense, US Navy, Photographer's Mate 3rd Class Larry Carlson; p. 31, bottom: TANG CHHIN SOTHY/AFP/Getty Images; p. 32: © AP Photo/KEYSTONE/Georgios Kefalas; p. 35: © Vaun Jordan; pp. 38, 39: © Perry Michael.

Library of Congress Cataloging-in-Publication Data
Goodman, Susan E.
Motorcycles! / by Susan E. Goodman and Michael J. Doolittle. — 1st ed.
    p.   cm. — (Step into reading step 3 book)
ISBN 978-0-375-84116-3 (trade) — ISBN 978-0-375-94116-0 (lib. bdg.)
1. Motorcycles—Juvenile literature. 2. Motorcycling—Juvenile literature. I. Doolittle, Michael J.
II. Title.   TL440.15.G66 2007   629.227'5—dc22   2006101199

Printed in the United States of America   10 9 8 7 6 5 4 3 2 1   First Edition

Motorcycles!

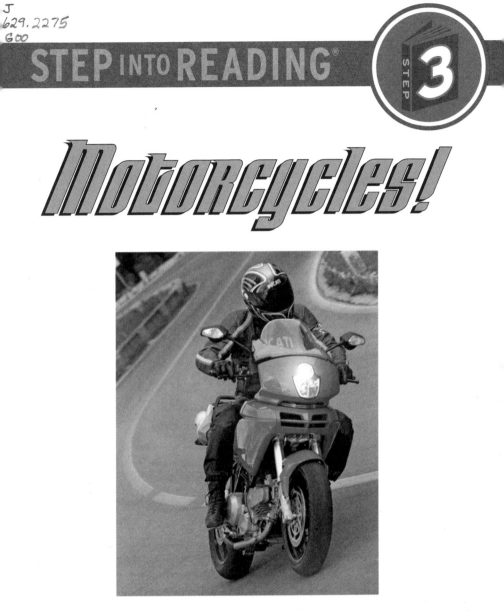

By Susan E. Goodman

Photographs taken and selected by
Michael J. Doolittle

Random House 🏠 New York

Amazing Cycles

The crowd is quiet.

All eyes are on Robbie Knievel.

He is about to risk his life.

Robbie is a

motorcycle stunt jumper.

His father, Evel Knievel,

jumped over this fountain in 1968.

But he crashed.

He almost died.

It is Robbie's turn to try.

Robbie revs his engine.

He shoots off a ramp

at 95 miles an hour.

He's flying!

Robbie aims

for the landing ramp.

From so high up,

it looks like a Popsicle stick.

He makes it!

The crowd cheers.

Over the next few years,

Robbie will jump over trucks, jets,

even the Grand Canyon!

Cycles, motorbikes, bikes.
Whatever you call them,
motorcycles are awesome.
And you do not have to be
a stunt jumper to ride one.

Motorcycles come
in many shapes and sizes.
Touring bikes
are a comfortable way
to ride on two wheels!

Sport bikes are
smaller and faster.

And choppers?

Choppers are just cool!

Fast and Faster

What can you do

on a motorcycle?

You can go fast.

Racing bikes are light,

but their engines are

big and powerful.

They can race at more than

200 miles an hour.

You can go even faster!

Some motorcycles

look like rockets.

They are built to set

speed records.

They fly by

at over 330 miles an hour!

You can take a trip

on a motorcycle.

Emilio Scotto did.

His trip was ten years long!

He visited 214 countries.

He used 11,000 gallons of gas.

He wore out 86 tires.

Most riders take shorter trips.
Some bikers just like to go
on rides with their friends.

Or their animal friends.

Even their

stuffed-animal friends!

Boneshakers

In 1885,

Gottlieb Daimler invented

the gas engine.

He put it on a machine

that looked like a bicycle.

It was made of wood.

Even the wheels were wooden!

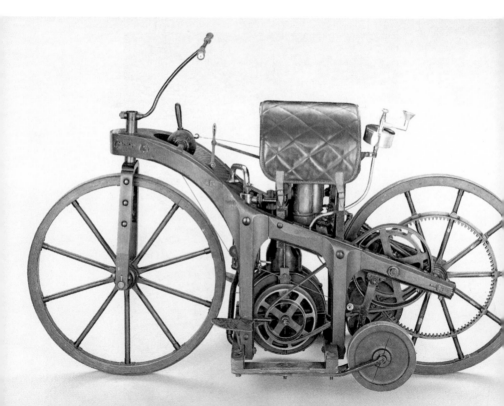

Daimler's son Paul tested it.
He zoomed off
at seven miles an hour.
This nine-year-old was
the world's first motorcycle rider!
But early motorcycles were not
very comfortable.

They did not have springs.
They bumped over bad roads.
No wonder they were called
"boneshakers"!

Here are the parts of a motorcycle:

hand brake

handlebars

headlight

fender

rim

shift lever

foot peg

engine

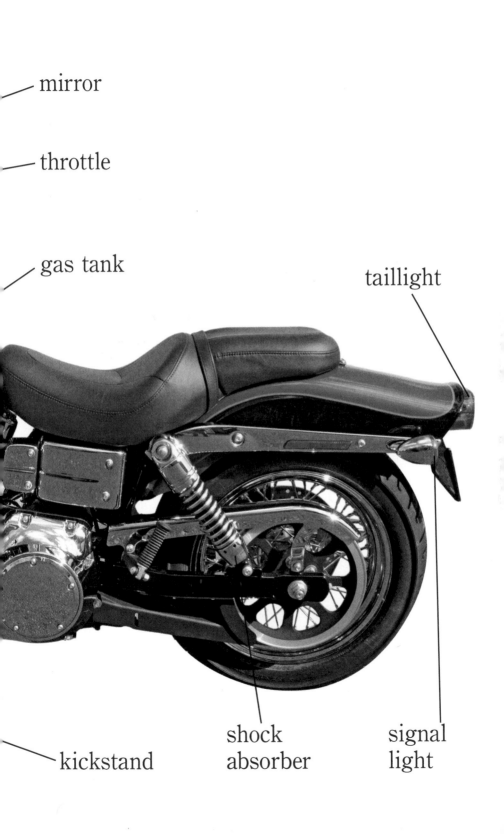

mirror

throttle

gas tank

taillight

kickstand

shock
absorber

signal
light

How do motorcycles work?
The engine makes
the back wheel move.
You turn the throttle
to make the bike speed up.

You squeeze the brake
to slow it down.

You steer a motorcycle
just like you steer a bicycle.
You move the handlebars.
To turn a corner,
you must also lean.

Riders wear special gear
to stay safe.

A helmet protects your head.

Leather jackets protect you

from cuts and scrapes if you fall.

Goggles and visors

keep dust out of your eyes.

Bugs too!

Motorcycles at Work

Not long ago,

a boy in an African village

ran to his father.

"Mother is sick," he said.

The nearest doctor was

miles away.

The woman could not walk.

A motorcycle with a stretcher

became her ambulance.

She got help in time.

Motorcycles can go places
that cars and trucks cannot.
So they can do
many different jobs.
In the country,
some farmers use them
to round up cattle.

In the city,
police weave through traffic
to stop speeding cars.
They dart into alleys
to catch crooks.

Soldiers began using motorcycles
long ago.
Some of their bikes
had three wheels.
They looked like
a motorcycle and a car
rolled into one.
The extra part was called
a sidecar.
One soldier drove the motorcycle.
Another sat in the sidecar.

Soldiers still use motorcycles.
Ships and helicopters
carry the bikes to war zones.
Soldiers ride them in deserts
and over mountain trails.

Motorcycles take people
to work.
In some countries,
they are rebuilt
so many people can ride.

Santa's helpers can use
motorcycles to go to work too.
They do not have reindeer.
So they become Cycle Santas
and deliver gifts.
That might be the best job
a motorcycle can have!

Making a Bike Your Own

Many riders want to make
their bikes special.

Some folks build big bikes
for traveling.

This one looks like a boat.

But this fisherman

brings his real boat along.

Some bikers like to ride
their motorcycles in the snow.
One rider turned his bike
into a snow-cycle!

Some people like to decorate

their motorcycles.

They get new tires.

They put on fancy rims,

or add flashing lights.

Then there are fun paint jobs.

One man's bike looks like
a rattlesnake!

Its tail wraps around
the back wheel.
Its fangs seem ready to strike.

"This motorcycle is a painting that moves," he says.

Motocross!

It is almost time
for the first race.
Motocross races are on
dirt tracks with hills,
bumps, and turns.
Motocross is the most popular
kind of motorcycle racing.
Kids can do it too.

Motocross bikes are built
to ride on rough ground.
Their engines are set up high
to avoid rocks.
Strong springs make
riding over bumps easier.
Knobby tires grip the trail.

The kids line up for the race.
One father checks
his son's helmet.

Another dad double-checks
his son's brakes.

Three . . . two . . . one . . . Go!

The racers speed off

as fast as they can.

They all want to be in the lead.

They zoom around a sharp turn.

Some racers slow down.

Some put their foot down

to keep from tipping over.

This race is six laps long.

Riders pass each other.

They zigzag to avoid ruts.

They rush up steep hills.

Some soar 15 feet in the air

before landing.

The winner streaks across
the finish line.

The racers keep coming in
until everyone has finished.
But all of the kids are winners.
Because riding motorcycles
is fun!

CCDC AS 1/08

CCDC 3/08